EARTH

by Ruth Owen

WINDMILL
BOOKS

New York

Published in 2014 by Windmill Books, An Imprint of Rosen Publishing
29 East 21st Street, New York, NY 10010

Produced for Windmill by Ruby Tuesday Books Ltd
Editor for Ruby Tuesday Books Ltd: Mark J. Sachner
US Editor: Joshua Shadowens
Designer: Alix Wood
Consultant: Kevin Yates, Fellow of the Royal Astronomical Society

Photo Credits:
Cover, 6–7, 8–9, 11 (bottom), 12, 14, 16, 18–19, 24–25, 26–27 © Shutterstock; 1, 4–5, 10–11, 17, 21, 22–23, 28–29 © NASA; 13 © Science Photo Library; 15, 18 (bottom) © Ruby Tuesday Books; 20 © Wikipedia Creative Commons.

Publisher Cataloging Data

Owen, Ruth.
Earth / by Ruth Owen.
   p. cm. — (Explore outer space)
Includes index.
ISBN 978-1-61533-724-8 (library binding) — ISBN 978-1-61533-765-1 (pbk.) —
 ISBN 978-1-61533-766-8 (6-pack)
1. Earth (Planet) — Juvenile literature. I. Owen, Ruth, 1967-. II. Title.
QB631.4 O94 2014
550—dc23

Manufactured in the United States of America

CPSIA Compliance Information: Batch #BS13WM: For Further Information contact Windmill Books, New York, New York at 1-866-478-0556

CONTENTS

OUR HOME IN THE SOLAR SYSTEM

A visitor from outer space approaching Earth, with its blue waters, green and brown landmasses, and white, cloudy **atmosphere**, would view a swirl of color against the blackness of space.

Upon landing, that visitor would find a world unlike any of the other seven **planets** or millions of other objects that **orbit** our Sun. Like other worlds in our **solar system**, Earth has a mixture of chemicals that produce landforms, an atmosphere, weather patterns, and various kinds of liquids and gases. But nowhere else in the solar system do all these **elements** come together to produce the incredible variety of features we have on Earth.

Earth is also the only world in our solar system where, so far, any form of life is known to exist. And even more amazingly, Earth is the only planet we know of in the **universe**, again, so far, where the kind of intelligent life exists that makes it possible for you to be reading this book!

Earth

This view of Earth became known as the "Pale Blue Dot." It was captured by the *Voyager 1* spacecraft in 1990. *Voyager 1* was 4 billion miles (6.4 billion km) from Earth, heading for the outer reaches of the solar system.

Our beautiful Earth seen from space.

That's Out of This World!

It has only been since 1992 that scientists have actually detected planets beyond our own solar system. Since then, hundreds of these planets, known as **exoplanets**, have been found. Today, astronomers estimate that there are probably hundreds of billions of exoplanets just in our **galaxy**, the **Milky Way**.

THE BIRTH OF OUR SOLAR SYSTEM

Earth and the other planets in the solar system were created when our Sun formed about 4.5 billion years ago.

Before the solar system came into being, there was a huge cloud of gas and dust in space. Over time, the cloud collapsed on itself. Most of the gas and dust formed a massive spinning sphere, or ball. As the sphere spun in space, a disk formed, around the sphere, from the remaining gas and dust. As all this matter rotated, the sphere pulled in more gas and dust, adding to its size, weight, and **gravity**. The pressure of all the material pressing onto the center of the sphere caused the center to get hotter and hotter. Finally, the temperature inside the sphere got so hot that the sphere ignited to become a new star. That star was our Sun!

Leftover gas and dust continued to spin in a disk around the Sun. Over time, this matter clumped together to form eight planets, including our Earth, the planets' moons, and smaller objects such as **dwarf planets**, and **asteroids**.

That's Out of This World!

Mercury, Venus, Earth, and Mars are the planets that formed closest to the Sun. All four planets have solid, rocky surfaces. They are known as the terrestrial planets. The word terrestrial comes from the Latin word terra, which means "earth" or "land."

EARTH AND ITS PLACE IN SPACE

For around 4.5 billion years, the planets in our solar system have been orbiting the Sun, each taking its own path, or orbit, around our star.

Five of the solar system's planets, Mercury, Venus, Mars, Jupiter, and Saturn, can be seen in the sky with the naked eye, so were known about from earliest times.

In March 1781, British astronomer Sir William Herschel observed Uranus for the first time. At first, he thought he'd seen a **comet**. In September 1846, German astronomer Johann Gottfried Galle discovered Neptune.

Then, in 1930, American astronomer Clyde Tombaugh discovered a tiny, distant planet, which was named Pluto. For decades, therefore, our solar system was home to nine planets. In 2007, however, the International Astronomical Union reclassified Pluto as a dwarf planet because of its small size. Also, Pluto does not have the gravitational power to "sweep up" all the objects close to it and pull them into its orbit, like the eight larger "true" planets.

Sun

This diagram shows our solar system. The planets' sizes in relation to each other and the distances between them are not to scale.

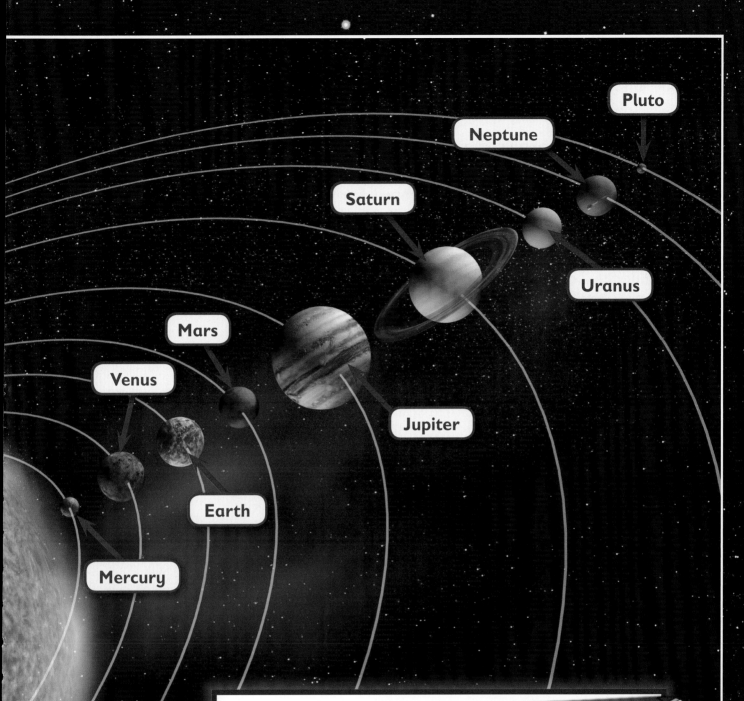

Pluto

Neptune

Saturn

Uranus

Mars

Venus

Jupiter

Earth

Mercury

That's Out of This World!

The Romans named the planets Mercury, Venus, Mars, Jupiter, and Saturn after their gods. Much later, when Uranus, Neptune, and the dwarf planet Pluto were discovered, these planets were also named for ancient Roman or Greek gods. Our planet has been called Earth for about 1,000 years. Its name comes from the Old English word, ertha, which simply means "the ground."

EARTH'S STAR

Earth continually orbits the Sun at an average distance of about 93 million miles (150 million km) away. That distance is very important for our planet because it means we are in a zone that scientists sometimes call "the Goldilocks Zone."

The Goldilocks Zone gets its name because at this distance from the Sun, it is neither too hot nor too cold. The "just right" temperatures and conditions inside the zone mean Earth is able to support liquid water, which is essential for living things to develop and stay alive.

As a star, our Sun is not particularly special, and it has no unusual features. Like the billions of other stars in the Milky Way, it is just a burning ball of hydrogen and helium gases. It's very easy, in fact, to take the Sun's energy for granted. Without the Sun's light and heat, however, we could not exist on our home planet.

That's Out of This World!

It's impossible to imagine the quantity of energy that the Sun produces, but here's one way to look at it. Take the amount of energy used in the United States in one year, multiply it by one million, and that's how much energy the Sun produces every second!

Light from the Sun takes about eight minutes to reach Earth. So we always see what happened on the Sun eight minutes ago!

As the Sun burns, it releases pieces of atoms, known as atomic particles, into space. When these particles enter Earth's atmosphere at the North and South Poles, they create beautiful, colorful light shows called "aurora" high in the sky.

EARTH'S DAYS AND YEARS

We call the time period that it takes a planet to make one full orbit of the Sun a year. Earth orbits the Sun once every 365 days, so a year on Earth is 365 days.

To make one full orbit of the Sun, Earth travels a distance of 584 million miles (940 million km). It is moving through space at an average speed of 66,622 miles per hour (107,218 km/h).

At the same time as orbiting the Sun, Earth is also spinning, or rotating, on its **axis**. It makes one full rotation every 24 hours.

The Earth doesn't spin completely upright because its axis is slightly tilted at 23.5 degrees. As the planet moves around the Sun, this tilt causes Earth to have different seasons. When the planet's northern **hemisphere** is tilted towards the Sun, the north has summer and the south has winter. When the southern hemisphere tilts towards the Sun, the south has summer and the north has winter.

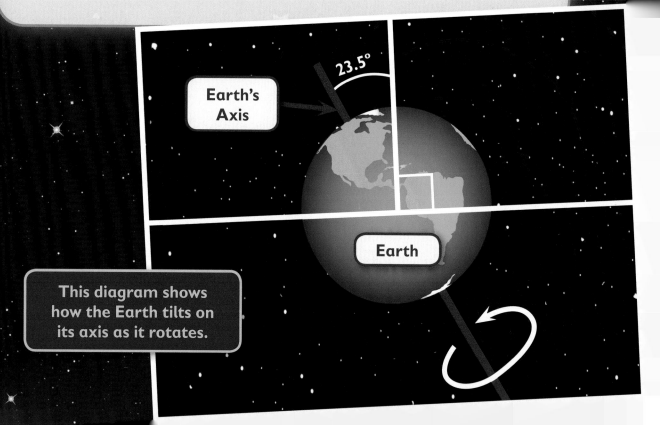

23.5°

Earth's Axis

Earth

This diagram shows how the Earth tilts on its axis as it rotates.

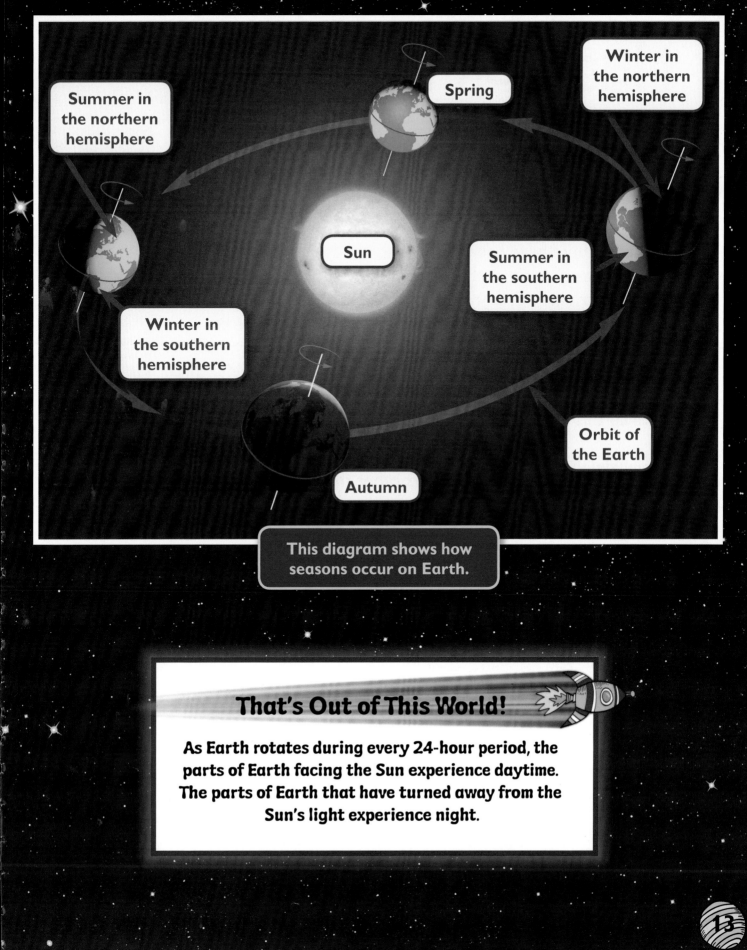

Summer in the northern hemisphere

Spring

Winter in the northern hemisphere

Sun

Summer in the southern hemisphere

Winter in the southern hemisphere

Orbit of the Earth

Autumn

This diagram shows how seasons occur on Earth.

That's Out of This World!

As Earth rotates during every 24-hour period, the parts of Earth facing the Sun experience daytime. The parts of Earth that have turned away from the Sun's light experience night.

THE MOON: OUR NEAREST NEIGHBOR IN SPACE

Traveling through space at an average distance of about 238,855 miles (384,400 km) from Earth is the Moon. As Earth orbits the Sun, the Moon is orbiting Earth. It makes one full orbit of our planet every 27.3 days.

Over the years there have been many theories as to how the Moon formed. One theory was that the Moon formed alongside the Earth from material left over from the birth of the Sun. Today, most scientists believe a planet, or some other space body, the size of Mars crashed into Earth soon after it formed. Superheated chunks of Earth and the impactor planet flew out into space. Over time this debris clumped together to form the Moon, which has continued to orbit Earth to this day.

Our Moon has one very important claim to fame. Its rocky, dusty surface is the only place in the universe, other than Earth, where a human has ever stood!

Earth

Mars-sized
impactor planet

This artwork shows how rock from Earth
may have formed the Moon following an
impact with another planet.

That's Out of This World!

From Earth, we see the Moon seem to change shape, or go through different phases. Sometimes it is a thin crescent shape. At other times it's a giant, white disk. These changes happen because as the Moon orbits Earth, different parts of the Moon catch the Sun's light.

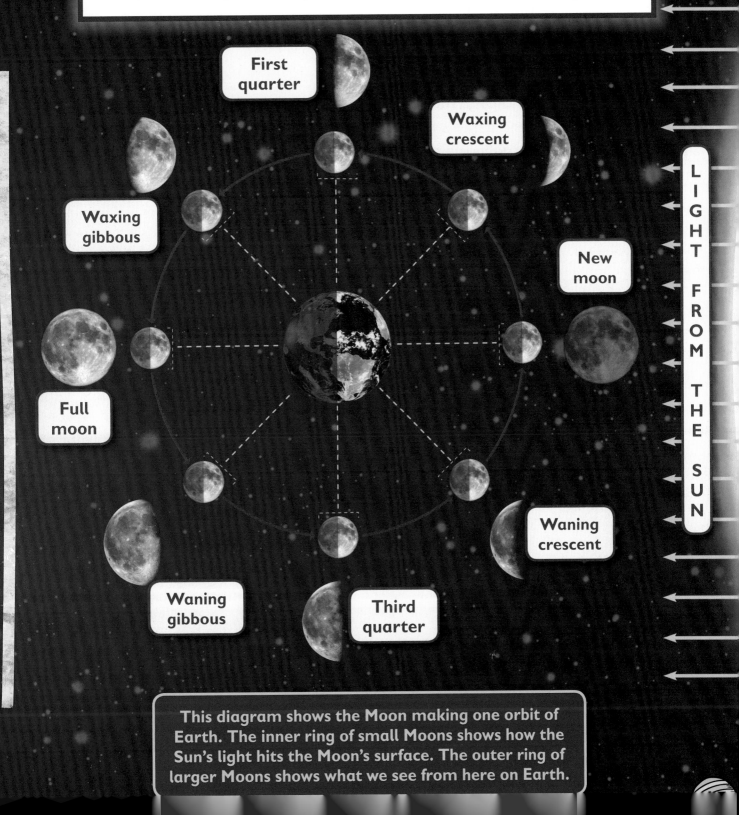

First quarter

Waxing crescent

Waxing gibbous

New moon

Full moon

Waning crescent

Waning gibbous

Third quarter

LIGHT FROM THE SUN

This diagram shows the Moon making one orbit of Earth. The inner ring of small Moons shows how the Sun's light hits the Moon's surface. The outer ring of larger Moons shows what we see from here on Earth.

EARTH, INSIDE AND OUT

Earth is made up of three layers called the crust, the mantle, and the core.

Where there is land, Earth's rocky crust is 15 to 35 miles (24–56 km) thick. Beneath the planet's oceans, the crust is just 3 to 5 miles (4.8–8 km) thick.

Below the crust is the mantle. The upper layer of the mantle is formed from rock. Beneath this rigid upper layer, however, it is so hot that rock actually melts and forms thick, oozing, **molten** rock called **magma**.

Deep inside the Earth is the core. The outer layer of the core is made of molten iron and nickel. Here, temperatures reach about 8,000°F (4,400°C). The inner core is a solid mass of metal with a temperature of around 9,000°F (5,000°C). That's as hot as the surface of the Sun!

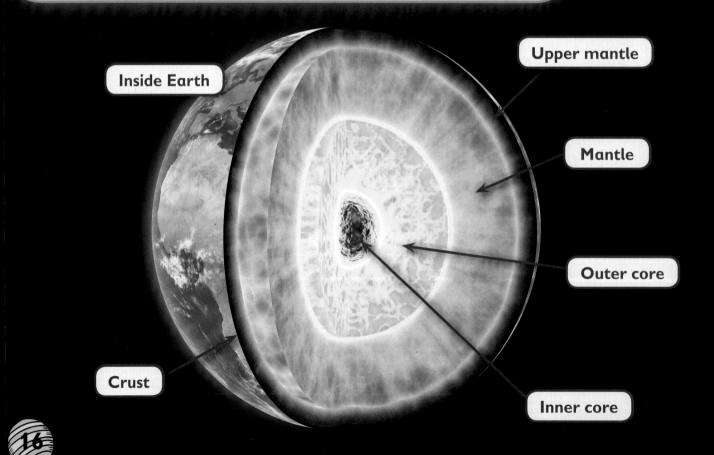

Inside Earth

Upper mantle

Mantle

Outer core

Crust

Inner core

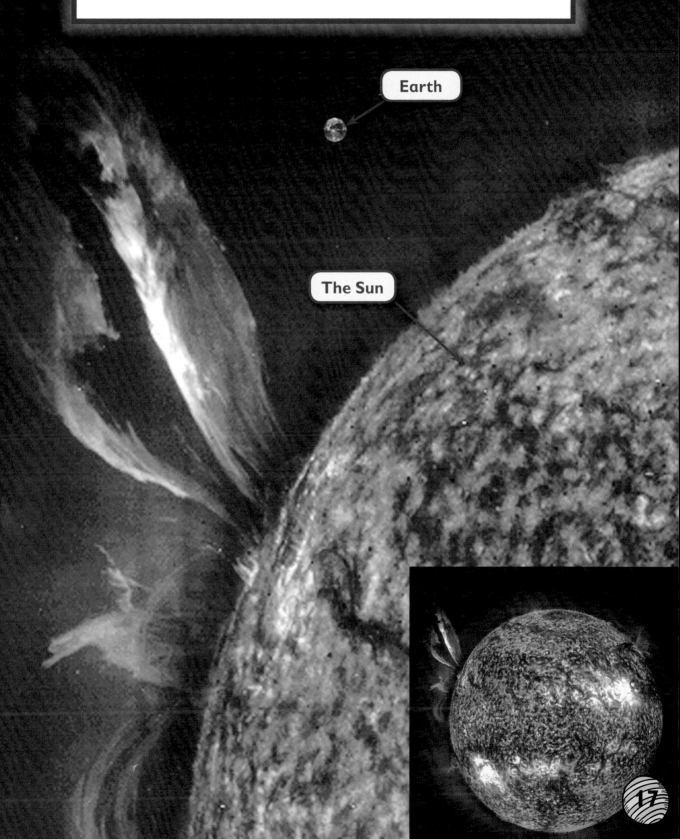

That's Out of This World!

Earth has a diameter of 7,918 miles (12,742 km). From our position here on Earth, our planet seems huge. Compared to the Sun and larger planets in the solar system, however, Earth is a very small space object indeed!

Earth

The Sun

17

OUR RESTLESS PLANET

Throughout the history of our planet, constant movements in the Earth's crust and flows of magma that burst onto the Earth's surface have been changing and shaping the look of our planet.

Earth's crust is broken into large pieces, called tectonic plates, that fit together like a giant jigsaw puzzle. The tectonic plates are constantly moving, which squeezes and stretches the rocks that make up the crust. One way that we see the results of these movements is when we look at ancient mountains. Often, the mountains will have formed when layers of rock rose up, buckling and folding over each other, on either side of a huge crack that appeared in the Earth's crust.

Sometimes, as the Earth's crust moves and cracks it allows magma from inside the mantle to come to the surface. The magma flows over the ground. Then it cools and hardens, forming layers of new rock, and creating a new landscape.

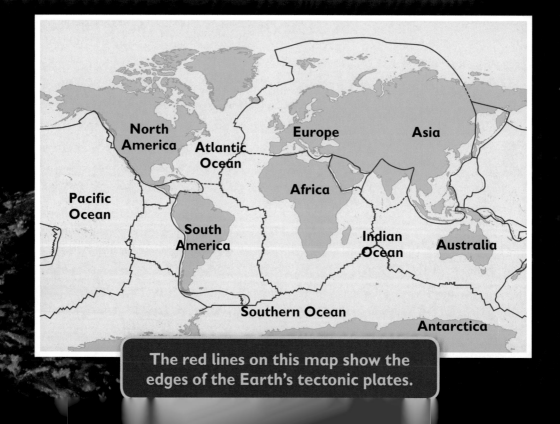

North America
Atlantic Ocean
Europe
Asia
Pacific Ocean
Africa
South America
Indian Ocean
Australia
Southern Ocean
Antarctica

The red lines on this map show the edges of the Earth's tectonic plates.

That's Out of This World!

We sometimes see magma erupt from a volcano. A volcano is a hollow mountain that provides a pathway from the Earth's mantle to the surface of the planet. When a volcano erupts, the magma, or **lava**, that flows down its slopes cools and hardens, changing the mountain's shape and making it grow larger.

Magma, or lava, bursts from a volcano onto the Earth's surface.

EARTH'S ROCKY SURFACE

Like the other terrestrial planets in the solar system, Earth's surface is covered in a wide variety of rocky features including mountains, volcanoes, and **canyons**.

The tallest mountain on Earth is Mount Everest. Standing nearly 5.5 miles (8.8 km) high, Earth's record-breaking mountain is part of the Himalayas **mountain range** on the border of China and Nepal, in Asia.

At 6.3 miles (10.2 km) high, the inactive volcano, Mauna Kea, which forms part of the island of Hawaii, is actually taller than Mount Everest. Only the top 2.6 miles (4.2 km) of this giant is above **sea level**, however, and the heights of mountains are always officially measured above sea level.

Earth's longest **mountain chain** is the Andes. The mountains stretch along the west coast of South America for about 5,500 miles (8,800 km). The mountain chain was formed about 70 million years ago by the collision of two of Earth's tectonic plates.

Earth's tallest mountain, Mount Everest, viewed from a plane.

That's Out of This World!

One of Earth's most famous and amazing natural landscape features is the Grand Canyon in Arizona. The canyon was carved from the surrounding rock by the flowing waters of the Colorado River. The canyon is 277 miles (446 km) long and up to 18 miles (29 km) wide. In places, it is a mile (1.6 km) deep.

EARTH'S PROTECTIVE ATMOSPHERE

Earth's atmosphere is a protective blanket of gases that surround our planet at heights up to 75 miles (120 km) above the planet's surface.

The atmosphere is made up of 78 percent nitrogen, 21 percent oxygen, and 1 percent other gases.

By day, Earth's atmosphere stops the planet from becoming too hot. At night, the layer of gases stores daytime heat, keeping the planet warm. This stored heat prevents temperatures from dropping as they do on the planet Mercury, which has no atmosphere. At night, with no stored heat to warm the planet, temperatures on Mercury plummet to −280°F (−173°C)!

Earth's atmosphere also absorbs dangerous rays from the Sun and protects our world from objects such as small **meteoroids** and asteroids that are on a collision course with Earth. As rocky space objects head for our planet, they enter the protective atmosphere and are burned up or broken into smaller pieces that rarely cause damage when they hit the Earth's surface.

This is the view from the surface of Mercury. The planet has no atmosphere so the blackness of space can be seen day and night.

That's Out of This World!

The Sun's light is made up of different colors. Earth's atmosphere scatters the Sun's light, allowing mostly blue light waves through. This is why Earth's daytime sky looks blue. Without our atmosphere, our sky would be like that of Mercury, with nothing but the blackness of space, day and night.

The Moon

Earth's atmosphere

Earth

THE BLUE PLANET

You may have heard people describe our planet as "the blue planet." This is because about 70 percent of Earth's surface is covered with water, and from space, the planet looks blue.

We are probably most familiar with water in its liquid state, but it also exists as a solid, when frozen, or as a gas called water vapor, when it evaporates. Liquid water is found on Earth in the oceans, in lakes, in rivers and streams, and even underground. Water as solid ice exists on mountain tops, in **glaciers**, and in the polar ice caps, which are huge sheets of ice at the North and South Poles. Water vapor is in the air all around us.

Water plays a huge role in the life of our planet. Over half of the **species** of animals, plants, and other life forms that inhabit our planet live in water. And of those species that do not live in water, all of them require water in some form in order to stay alive.

Even in the very coldest oceans on Earth, life exists!

That's Out of This World!

Water changes its form from liquid to gas and back to liquid or solid ice as it moves through a natural global cycle called the **water cycle**. The quantity of water on Earth and in our atmosphere never changes. In fact, all the water on Earth has been here since our planet's earliest days, moving through the water cycle again, and again, and again.

The Water Cycle

Water drops gather together and form rain clouds. In very cold air, water drops may freeze and become snow.

Water vapor rises high in the sky where it is cold. The vapor condenses and forms water drops.

Rain and snow fall from clouds back to Earth. Some water may freeze and spend a period of time as ice on Earth.

Water in oceans, lakes, rivers, and even puddles is warmed by the Sun. It evaporates and becomes a gas called water vapor.

Rainwater and melted snow and ice run into rivers, which eventually run into the ocean.

LIFE ON EARTH

Life is one of the things that makes Earth unique among all the planets in our solar system.

Today astronomers and other scientists are closer than they have ever been to figuring out if there is any chance that even the smallest, simplest **organisms** may ever have existed in other parts of the solar system. Even if such evidence turns up, however, we can be pretty sure that no other world orbiting our Sun has ever had the incredible variety and complexity of life forms that we enjoy on Earth.

Earth is home to microscopic bacteria that live inside our bodies and in parts of the Earth that are so hot or cold as to seem uninhabitable. It is also home to mammals, birds, reptiles, insects, spiders, and about half a million different types of plants. Scientists are not in complete agreement about how many different kinds of life are on Earth today. Some estimate, however, that there may be as many as 8.7 million entirely different species!

That's Out of This World!

The very simplest forms of life began appearing on our planet around 3.5 billion years ago.

OTHER EARTHS: ARE WE ALONE?

For centuries, humans have wanted to know if life exists, and in particular, intelligent life, in other parts of the universe. Could there be another Earthlike planet out there? Is it possible that we are not alone?

While astronomers have been able to observe stars beyond our solar system for centuries, it was too difficult to see if there were planets orbiting those stars.

In March 2009, the Kepler space observatory, which carries a powerful telescope, was launched. Kepler's mission is to study part of the Milky Way and look for exoplanets. In particular, the mission is hoping to discover planets that are orbiting their stars in the Goldilocks Zone, where there is liquid water and temperatures are neither too hot nor too cold and a planet could support life!

By the beginning of 2013, Kepler scientists had confirmed the discovery of over 100 planets, and nearly 3,000 objects that might be planets. While confirmation that another Earth exists is yet to come, perhaps one day soon we will get an answer to the question: Are we alone?

That's Out of This World!

The Kepler telescope monitors the brightness of stars and then looks for any sign of the star's light dimming because an object, such as a planet, has passed in front of the star. Kepler is so powerful that it could look down on Earth and detect the dimming of a porch light as somebody passed in front of it!

Earth

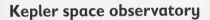

Kepler space observatory

GLOSSARY

asteroids (AS-teh-roydz) Rocky objects orbiting the Sun and ranging in size from a few feet (m) to hundreds of miles (km) in diameter.

atmosphere (AT-muh-sfeer) The layer of gases surrounding a planet, moon, or star.

axis (AK-sus) An imaginary line about which a body, such as a planet, rotates.

canyons (KAN-yunz) Deep, rocky valleys.

comet (KAH-mit) An object orbiting the Sun consisting primarily of a center of ice and dust and, when they near the Sun, tails of gas and dust particles pointing away from the Sun.

dwarf planets (DWAHRF PLA-nets) Objects in space that look and act like planets but are much smaller and do not have enough gravity to pull all the other objects close to them into their orbit.

elements (EH-luh-ments) Chemical substances that consist of only one type of atom and cannot be broken down into simpler substances by a chemical reaction.

exoplanets (ek-soh-PLA-nets) Planets outside of our solar system.

galaxy (GA-lik-see) A group of stars, dust, gas, and other objects held together in outer space by gravity.

glaciers (GLAY-shurz) Huge, slow-moving masses, or sheets, of ice.

gravity (GRA-vuh-tee) The force that causes objects to be attracted toward Earth's center or toward other physical bodies in space, such as stars, planets, and moons.

hemisphere (HEH-muh-sfeer) A half of a planet or other astronomical body, divided either into northern and southern halves by the equator or into eastern and western halves by an imaginary line passing through the north and south poles.

lava (LAH-vuh) Rock that has been heated within a planet, moon, or asteroid to the point where it flows like a liquid.

magma (MAG-muh) Underground rock that has become so hot it melts.

meteoroids (MEE-tee-uh-roydz) Small particles or fragments that have broken free from an asteroid.

Milky Way (MIL-kee WAY) The galaxy that includes Earth and the rest of our Sun's solar system.

molten (MOHL-ten) Melted, or liquefied, by heat.

mountain chain (MOWN-tun CHAYN) A line of mountains made up of more than one mountain range.

mountain range (MOWN-tun RAYNJ) A group of mountains.

orbit (OR-bit) Circle around another object in a curved path.

organisms (OR-guh-nih-zuhmz) Living things.

planets (PLA-nets) Objects in space that are of a certain size and that orbit, or circle, a star.

sea level (SEE LEH-vul) The surface of the sea. It is used as a starting point for measuring the height of land and mountains.

solar system (SOH-ler SIS-tem) The Sun and everything that orbits around it, including asteroids, meteoroids, comets, and the planets and their moons.

species (SPEE-sheez) One type of living thing. The members of a species look alike and can produce young together.

universe (YOO-nih-vers) All of the matter and energy that exists as a whole, including gravity and all the planets, stars, galaxies, and contents of intergalactic space.

water cycle (WAH-ter SY-kul) The process in which water evaporates and moves from Earth up into the sky as water vapor, condenses into water drops to form clouds, and falls back to Earth again as rain or snow.

WEBSITES

For web resources related to the subject of this book, go to: www.windmillbooks.com/weblinks and select this book's title.

READ MORE

Allyn, Daisy. *Earth: The Blue Planet*. Our Solar System. New York: Gareth Stevens Leveled Readers, 2010.

Ballard, Carol. *Earth and the Solar System*. Earth and Space Science. Mankato, MN: Raintree, 2010.

Oilen, Rebecca. *Exploring Earth*. Objects in the Sky. New York: PowerKids Press, 2007.

INDEX